101
WAYS
TO
HAPPINESS

101 WAYS TO HAPPINESS

MIKE ANNESLEY

SIRIUS

For Manon

SIRIUS

This edition published in 2020 by Sirius Publishing, a division of
Arcturus Publishing Limited,
26/27 Bickels Yard, 151–153 Bermondsey Street,
London SE1 3HA

ISBN: 978-1-3988-0189-9
AD007307UK

Printed in China

All images courtesy of Shutterstock.

CONTENTS

CHAPTER THREE

HAPPILY WORKING 143

INTRODUCTION

"Are you happy?" The question might to some people seem naive or unreal – like "Have you found the secret of eternal life?"

To answer, you might need to stop and think a while. Some might say "Yes, I'm happy … with reservations." This is a good response. Anyone who can offer it sincerely is well placed to live a fulfilling life. For you, if you fall into this category, the purpose of this book is to indicate that maybe you're even happier than you might imagine; and that further happiness might be available if you're prepared to put a little thought into how you can tackle your challenges more effectively, make some adjustments to your lifestyle or attitudes and seize some of the opportunities that are there for taking.

If you're among those who answer, "No, unfortunately I can't claim to be happy," you've plenty to look forward to. This book is for you as well. Perhaps you're looking at life through grey-tinted spectacles. Perhaps you have an elevated idea of happiness as continual joy, putting a perpetual smile on your face. To have a more realistic view of what happiness consists

of is not to underrate its life-transforming impact. Whether your answer is *yes with reservations* or *no, not at all*, the insights offered here are designed to give you a heightened sense of well-being that is well within your grasp if you're open to new ways of thinking and living. These are the ways to happiness – the pathways for you to explore. Just try, say, half a dozen of them initially: you'll soon notice the difference.

Positive change

None of these pathways will require you to set out on a long, arduous trek. You won't need to travel that far to find and follow them. They are largely about discovering in yourself and in your life the precious gifts that already reside there, hidden.

It's true you'll need to embrace certain changes. But the benefits of making such changes will mostly be self-evident. They'll be even more obvious once you've taken your first steps along a particular pathway. You can make your journey in stages. You'll have no regrets – no wish to return to base camp and snuggle up in your sleeping bag.

You're tremendously blessed, already. This is true of anyone with a fair amount of comfort and good fortune in their lives – somewhere to live, a reasonable level of health, a family, no shortage of food, a few friends, maybe a job. Waking up to the blessings you already possess, including the wealth of opportunities awaiting you, and the capacity you have for making the best of them, is the underlying theme of most of the pathways here.

Awakening

"Sleeping bag ... waking up." The choice of metaphors is deliberate. Wakefulness is all. To be fully awake is to be fully aware – now, in the moment. If you can attain a more mindful state of consciousness, you'll inevitably gain in self-knowledge, and once this has happened you'll be well placed to make carefully considered changes about the way you want to live. You'll be able to grow out of any negative thinking and damaging behaviour, replacing these with positive approaches you already know will make a difference to your quality of life – your happiness.

At the moment, in some aspects of your life, you're probably snoozing – on the threshold of a new day. Wake up fully now and decide which of the 101 ways you want to try first. Morning has broken ...

CHAPTER ONE

HAPPILY YOURSELF

We're happiest when fully ourselves. This means two things: resisting peer pressure, which pushes us toward conformity; and dealing with any confidence issues stemming from low self-esteem. Encouraging your true self to emerge and flourish is a letting go – of self-criticism, of low expectations, of habits of avoidance and self-protection. That will open the way for discovering your true potential. "Self-love" may sound narcissistic but in fact is precisely what's needed: to give due thought to your own well-being. Valuing yourself is the starting-point to finding the true value of everything that makes a life worthwhile.

"Pearls do not lie on the seashore. If you desire one you must dive for it."

CHINESE PROVERB

BUILD CONFIDENCE

To be confident is to know the value of your authentic self and be unafraid to project that self to others. Affirmations help (see overleaf), and there are three principles of acceptance to follow: don't worry about your physical appearance; accept and learn from your mistakes; assume that things won't always go to plan. In conversation, stick with what you know: prepare thoroughly if it's an interview. Try to be relaxed in your confidence style: open to ideas, to criticism, and willing to change your goals.

Affirmations

Here are some confidence-building affirmations. Spend at least half a minute repeating each of these sentences slowly to yourself, and inhabiting them mentally. Create your own variations.

- I am myself, and no one else. I will let my qualities shine

- I will do my best, in my own way, and that is plenty

- I will be mindfully responsive to whatever happens

OUTWIT YOUR DEMONS

Demons are habitual responses that damage our inner peace – for example, difficulty in trusting a partner, caused by an ex-partner's behaviour. Fighting demons can lead to stress and obsession; fleeing from them often leads to drink or other harmful habits. Instead, get to know them. Forgive yourself for having them: self-compassion will shrink them. Make positive choices in life, based on self-awareness. Such choices will leave no space for your demons to do their mischief.

"What we resist, persists."

CARL JUNG

(3)

AVOID NEGATIVE SELF-TALK

Negative self-talk is self-fulfilling: you inwardly dwell on your faults, which makes you feel low, which leads you to perceive further faults. But you can refuse to listen. Treat these bad thoughts about yourself with mindful curiosity – and don't take them seriously. Stand back from them and be your best self.

ELIMINATE BAD HABITS

Bad habits undermine peace of mind. They may
go deep but should be tackled immediately.
Start with small lifestyle changes to make your
mental outlook more flexible and authentic
– for example, talk to strangers, try new leisure
pursuits, limit onscreen time. Avoid situations
that usually trigger your excesses: this might
mean spending less time with certain
friends. Scale down your worst habit in
stages; replace it with a new positive habit.
Do mindfulness meditation in order to
bring self-awareness to your efforts.

REACT, THEN RESPOND

It's useful to distinguish between reacting, which is instantaneous and often emotional, and responding, which is more considered and self-aware. Your mindful response to an event is always going to be more beneficial than your automatic reaction. When challenges present themselves, the instinctive reaction is often to want to flee from them, whereas the best response is to engage thoughtfully.

BE FLEXIBLE

Firmness of purpose is a strength, but can easily turn
to self-harming rigidity. Try to be open-minded, and
willing to change your views and objectives – though
not your most cherished values. By responding flexibly
to changing circumstances, you put yourself in a
good position to flourish. When trying to reaching a
conclusion, it helps if you can:

- Be willing to consider a situation without
  preconceptions

- Be open to opinions different from your own

- Be prepared to change your mind in the light of
  new evidence or thoughts

KNOW YOUR EMOTIONS

If you feel emotions bubbling, you might
be tempted to put a lid on them. Trying
to bottle them up never works: a blocked
emotion just builds up more pressure.
Allow yourself to feel your emotions fully
– then respond to them mindfully with a
thoughtful action plan. By all means let
off steam if it helps. Accepting the full
power of your emotions makes it easier
to move forward.

(8)

BALANCE PERSONAL NEEDS

Some deep needs are universal (comfort, love and so on); others are individual (for example, spending time in the mountains or stretching yourself creatively). Finding a way to satisfy your needs may be complicated by your work and family lives. It's essential to communicate your requirements well and be prepared to compromise. Contemplate the list of needs shown below and assess the relative importance of each: this is your compass to steer by.

- **Autonomy** – independence, freedom, resources
- **Comfort** – home, security, job
- **Connection** – family, friends, intimacy
- **Understanding** – learning, personal growth, education
- **Involvement** – neighbourhood, politics, volunteering
- **Recreation** – exercise, leisure, interests
- **Creativity** – talents, self-expression, home
- **Identity** – values, responsibilities, self-worth

PLAN PERSONAL GROWTH

Many of us live our inner lives on an *ad hoc* basis, taking each day as it comes. This can lead to drifting aimlessly, with general unease. Instead, with as much self-knowledge as you can muster, set a personal growth plan. We can all change, even radically, if we set our minds to it. Once you've identified a problem – be it procrastination, avoidance of intimate commitments or fear of self-exposure – it makes sense to eradicate it. Consciously take steps to follow a path of your own choosing. Be serious about yourself. Shape a growth plan and get started on the inner work that will take you where you want to go.

(10)

FIND MEANING IN YOUR LIFE

The "meaning of life" is a philosophical question – one you may never answer. However, it feels good to believe your own particular life has meaning, and this often follows from a sense of purpose. The Japanese speak of *ikigai*, or "reason for being": the thing that motivates you to get up in the mornings. Spend time on self-examination to find the purpose that shapes your life. Then look for opportunities to pursue that purpose. The most rewarding path is often to contribute to something greater than yourself.

(11)

LIVE YOUR VALUES

In tough times, it may seem harder to live by
your values — for example, money worries may
chip away at generosity. However, transgressing
against what you believe in will undermine
your self-worth. Know where your red lines are.
Talking about your values helps you to clarify
them — and going public puts pressure on you
to stay true to them. When temptation strikes,
ponder the *long-term* consequences of giving
way: keep yourself morally intact.

(12)

MANAGE YOUR ROLES

Every role we fill (mother, daughter, manager, friend) brings its own responsibilities, its demands on our time and energy. These will often clash. You can't completely satisfy everybody. Aim for something less than perfection – your best qualities will shine through without your aiming for the sky. Give what you can, in the best balance you can. Hang onto the essential you. This will help you in many roles, like motherhood: after all, mums set an example of how to live, not just provide nurture.

(13)

FORGIVE YOURSELF

Self-forgiveness is an important aspect of self-nurture. We all fall short of our own standards from time to time. We might not even realize we've done wrong until someone catches us out. Shame is an unhelpful emotion. By all means acknowledge guilt, but don't let it be a permanent shackle. Once you've offered any necessary apologies, and done your best to repair the situation, move on. Never let the past be an obstacle to a hopeful future.

(14)

CELEBRATE SUCCESSES

If you're working toward a personal goal, such as keeping up a fitness routine, studying a new skill or trying to be more confident in company, don't let any of your successes go unmarked. Congratulate yourself for each landmark passed. Share the good news with friends. Treat yourself – but if you're on a diet, make sure that treat doesn't break your self-imposed dietary rules!

(15)

ACCEPT YOUR BODY

Our relationship with our own body can be deeply
troubled. Many of us long to be taller, bustier, slimmer,
prettier, more muscular, or worry about signs of ageing.
Accepting your own body image is a vital part of
healthy self-compassion. Follow these principles
and be comfortable in your skin:

- Eat healthily and keep fit
- Reject fashionable norms and rejoice in individuality
- See the inner self as the thing that makes you
  attractive

VALUE YOUR MIND

Having a lower IQ than someone else
is rather like not being tall – it's a given.
Don't worry about this: IQ is an artificial
construct. Everyone has their own way
of being clever – their own permutation
of intuition, rationality, empathy,
imagination and creativity. Value your
mind for what it is, and use it to the full to
keep it nimble. So you're not a professor?
Neither are you President of the USA.
Accept who you are with pride.

KEEP FIT

If you can maintain good health and mobility,
your chances of being happy in later life are
hugely increased, but all too many of us demote
fitness to a low priority, especially when work
pressures impinge. Walk 10,000 steps daily if you
can. Do cardiovascular workouts for at least 20
minutes twice a week. Take the stairs instead
of the elevator whenever you've a chance. As
you age, don't overdo joint-straining exercise
such as running: marathons may not be for you.
Accustom yourself to treat moderate exercise as a
relaxing and essential part of your routine.

Beyond the gym

For those who find the gym too tame, here are some left-field exercise suggestions:

- Orienteering
- Wild swimming
- Woodland management
- Tandem cycling
- Latin dancing
- Indian dancing
- Kung fu
- Kickboxing

EAT AND DRINK WELL

Eating well is not just refuelling: as well as
calories you need a considered balance of
nutrients. Experts disagree but it's worth
navigating the maze of nutritional advice
and acting on informed conclusions.
Prioritize fruit and vegetables, snack only
on nuts, seeds and fruit, avoid processed
foods, simple (added) sugars and too
much salt. Controlling your diet (maybe
for ethical reasons as well as health) gives
extra purpose to your life. Drink alcohol and
caffeine-based drinks in moderation, if at all.
Avoid sugary drinks.

OPTIMIZE SLEEP

Sleeping better can enhance your memory and
concentration. Develop a pre-bedtime routine and stick to it.
Avoid caffeine, exercise or looking at a digital or TV screen
in the late evening. If you read in bed, opt for something
soothing – not crime fiction, psychological thrillers or
political analysis. Hug your partner and share the best
things that happened to you during the day.

PROTECT WHAT YOU TREASURE

It's self-evident: good things need to be keep safe.
But it's surprising how often this basic life rule
is broken. Be sure to recognize what's valuable.
Look after your body – your most precious
physical possession. Don't take for granted the
people who mean most to you. Nurture your
skills. Value your origins. And use your vote,
and ideally campaign, to ensure your values are
reflected in the political system you inhabit, at
local and national levels.

BE CREATIVE

Many feel they lack the artistic temperament. But creativity is at the core of our humanity. You can be creative without realizing it. Whenever you arrange pictures on a wall or choose fabrics for the home, you're letting your aesthetic instinct out to play. It's worth going further and seeing what happens if, say, you try making a vertical garden for your balcony from an old pallet or take a stab at drawing or assembling a collage or improvising a sculpture from found objects. Creativity follows no rules. Immerse yourself in making.

BE AGE-BLIND

Value people for who they are, regardless of age. Some of the
happiest friendships bridge generations. Shun social stereotyping
– the young as naive, the old as set in their ways. Relish the
illuminating wisdom often shown by kids; and joyful openness
in people with more life experience than you. Regard your own
physical signs of ageing as badges of honour, not landmarks on
a downhill track. Be as active as you can within the limitations
age imposes: don't overreach yourself.

CULTIVATE THE SPIRIT

The reality of the spirit is felt by people of different faiths – or no faith. It's the bond we share with all humankind. To value the spirit is to appreciate the mystery and beauty of creation. Deepen and extend your fulfilment, not by working to develop your spiritual side, but by dropping negative habits that inhibit its full blossoming. Believe in something beyond yourself – even if you can't name it or picture it. In times of difficulty, try the therapeutic power of prayer, which like meditation fosters well-being.

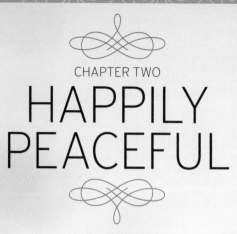

CHAPTER TWO

HAPPILY PEACEFUL

We all have our stresses and misfortunes to cope with, but that doesn't mean stress is the natural human condition. This chapter covers variations on two fundamental and complementary life skills: dealing with stress; and finding true peace. Included are some handy stress-busting quick fixes, as well as longer-term approaches to keep anxiety at bay. There's guidance too on lifestyle choices – everything from rationing your onscreen time to doing simple mindfulness meditations – that can coax peace into your everyday routines.

"Tension is who you think you should be.
Relaxation is who you are."

CHINESE PROVERB

BE MINDFUL

Mindfulness hasn't been overhyped: it genuinely offers an open sesame to inner peace. The idea is simple: cultivate the habit of giving full attention to the present moment, without judging yourself for any unwanted thoughts and feelings that may arise. When you notice your attention is distracted, gently return it to your chosen focus, which may be your breathing or bodily sensations, or some object like a fruit or ornament. You might benefit from a guided eight-week course but it's easy enough to go solo. Try the meditation on page 76, a classic mindfulness starting-point. Living more in the moment and less in the past and future detaches you from regrets and fears.

Mindful outcomes

As the basis for a meditation routine,
mindfulness brings the following benefits:

- **Thinking**
  Better memory, reaction times, intuition,
  concentration, decision-making

- **Well-being**
  Reduced anxiety and stress, relief from depression,
  control over bad habits, stronger immune system,
  improved cardiovascular health, better sleep

- **Fulfilment**
  Higher self-esteem, more confidence, better
  relationships, better focus on goals, release of
  personal potential

- **Self-awareness**
  Better self-knowledge, communication and
  management of emotions, enhanced empathy,
  better self-reliance and resilience

MAKE FRIENDS WITH TIME

We tend to treat time as a finite resource – a supply we can dip
into. Instead, focus on the *quality* of what you're doing, seeing time
as a neutral medium. Time is the vehicle of fulfilment, in the way
that the body is the vehicle of the soul. Clock time has its place in
family life and work but, whenever when you can, tune into your
body's natural cycles. Stop clock-watching. Good time management
is, it's true, a factor in *efficiency*: but sometimes effectiveness (which
means prioritizing the most worthwhile goals) is more *rewarding*.
Set directions as well as goals. Enjoy unplanned time. Avoid time
traps of your own making – commitments you can't fulfil.

(26)

MEDITATE

There's nothing esoteric or challenging about meditation –
any feeling that you may not be doing it right is against the
spirit of the practice. Meditate at least weekly. The benefits,
including enhanced awareness, sharper concentration and
reduced stress, will manifest gradually. Overleaf is a simple
mindfulness meditation that focuses on breathing.

A simple breath meditation

1 Sit comfortably in a kitchen or dining chair, feet flat on floor, legs uncrossed

2 Let your gaze fall about a metre (yard) in front of you, on the floor. Rest your hands on your thighs, palms down

3 Relax body and mind, keeping alert

4 Focus on your breath – the rise and fall of your belly, or air entering and leaving your nostrils

5 If your attention wanders, gently bring it back, without judging yourself for inattention

6 Finish after about 5 minutes. If you wish, use a timer

BE RESILIENT

There are two main foundation stones of
resilience – our ability to weather personal
storms. First, we must recognize situations
where the ego clings to the status quo because
that's more comfortable, and be prepared to let
go of such attachments; second, we must use
love and other cherished values as a compass
to take us through the storm. Don't expect to find
a cure for pain, whether physical or emotional.
But you can diminish its impact by recognizing
it for what it is: an *experience*, rather than the
essence of the self. Also, accepting impermanence
can help us to prepare for unwanted change,
lessening its harm when it hits us.

CONQUER STRESS

Stress is a hidden harm – it may go deeper than we realize, even threatening our health. But it needn't be this way. Take stress seriously and do what you can to expel it from your life. Ask yourself these questions:

- **Are there lifestyle changes I can make to keep stress at bay?**
  These might include working at home one day a week, saying no to extra commitments, sharing household jobs more equitably

- **Can I improve my responses to difficult situations?**
  Your natural mindset is peace, not tension. Maybe you are exaggerating your worries, misplacing your priorities, underrating your skill-set, not factoring in the support of loved ones?

- **Are there positive routines I can use to strengthen my mindset?**
  Possibilities include mindfulness meditation and yoga, sport, and personal projects that take you into the Zone

"The greatest weapon against stress is our ability to choose one thought over another."

WILLIAM JAMES

Two stress-busting quick fixes

Deploy these techniques whenever you feel the onset of stress or anxiety:

- **Four-by-four walking**
  Walk around in whatever space is available, following this count: breathe in for four steps, out for the next four, then in again, and so on. Keep this up for at least three minutes

- **A peace affirmation**
  Take a break from what you're doing. Ideally, sit down. Take a few slow, deep breaths. Say to yourself "I am ..." on the in-breath, then conclude " ... at peace" on the out-breath. Do this three or four times

LEARN TO SAY "NO"

Friendly people can find it hard to say no – to
extra tasks, changes put forward by others,
plans they don't, at heart, agree with. Saying yes
because it's easier can land you with undesirable
situations as well as lowering your self-esteem
by making yourself seem weak. Erecting a barrier
is sometimes a necessary self-defence measure.
This has nothing to do with closing off your
heart: only closing off your time. Say no – and
congratulate yourself for being clear and decisive.

MANAGE RISKS WELL

To stay permanently inside your comfort
zone would be a wasteful way to spend a life.
Fulfilment involves risk-taking. The best attitude
combines awareness with courage – even
relishing the challenge. Bear in mind you can
sometimes reduce risk by moving forward in
small steps. Transfer risk to others when you
can. If you decide a risk is too great, there are
two options: accept the status quo or find
a safer change. Be decisive about this.

(31)

USE YOUR INTUITION

Your intuition is an inner oracle. Contemplate its pronouncements
and see if you can frame them logically in words – that's a good
way to distinguish between intuition and the fearfulness prompted
by an anxious temperament. Sometimes intuition is drowned by
other peoples' voices, or by consciously collected evidence. So find
a quiet place where you can tune in to your inner voice of truth.

BREAK DOWN YOUR PROBLEMS

Catastrophizing is bundling up all your problems to make a mountain of many molehills. The opposite is healthier: breaking what may appear to be one issue down into smaller components and tackling these separately, in the right order. Find pathways through your problems. Taking the right pathway might automatically resolve a future difficulty, so you can cross that off your list too.

"The only thing that's the end of the world is the end of the world."

BARACK OBAMA

BE OPEN-MINDED

Whatever direction you're taking, it's good
to be open to ideas – even ones that alter
your direction dramatically. Rigid thinking can
lead you into error, so re-evaluate continuously.
You might find any by-ways you follow turn
into the main path. You might meet or hear
about someone whose ideas change your
whole approach. A word of warning: avoid
keeping your options open indefinitely
as a mask for procrastination.

ACCEPT THE UNKNOWN

Whatever intentions you set, the future remains unknown. The plans and mindsets of other people, and how well you can meet your own objectives, are both hidden from you. People with low self-esteem or poor levels of confidence will let their imagination loose on a prospect of failure, which may lead them to avoid risk – and get stuck in a rut. Think of the unknown as a place for creative interaction.

"People wish to be settled; only as far as they are unsettled is there any hope for them."

RALPH WALDO EMERSON

BE PLAYFUL

Play is not merely childlike exuberance: it's an attitude to life that revels in incongruity and absurdity and puts misfortune into a broader perspective. To be playful when faced with disappointment, loss or stressful change is to lift a courageous placard of resistance – to refuse to be cowed. Not every unwanted outcome is worth honouring with negative emotions. Being stoical in the face of adversity is admirable; a sprinkling of playfulness makes it even more so. And in relationships, play acknowledges the joy of being together.

(36)

FIND PEACE
IN MUSIC

Music can press many different
emotional buttons, including deeply
healing tranquillity. Even if your
preference is vibrant pop or rock, try
something peaceful as a tonic for
troubled times. Classical compositions
such as Debussy's *Clair de lune* or
Satie's *Trois gymnopédies* may fit the
bill. Experiment also with ambient
music (Brian Eno and Harold Budd
are worth exploring) and mind-body-
spirit sounds, composed specifically
for relaxation. Don't listen to relaxing
music while driving, as it can make
you dangerously dreamy!

Healing by ear

Here are two ideas for encouraging deep peace through sound:

- **Nature sounds**
  These work by combining a relaxing tempo with natural associations. Possibilities include: whale song; rain, river or ocean sounds; birdsong (especially the dawn chorus). Try online sources – there are plenty

- **Ragas**
  Classical India ragas, especially sitar and sarod recitals, are wonderfully restful. Each raga begins with a slow intro, called an alap, to get you in the mood. The tempo often builds to a virtuoso crescendo – relaxing because it takes you out of yourself. Try the sitar music of Anoushka Shankar, daughter of the great Ravi Shankar

CULTIVATE OPTIMISM

Optimistic people tend to be healthier as
well as happier – perhaps because they look
after themselves more. To be optimistic
you need to compartmentalize your larger
problems and treat mistakes as learning
opportunities. Winston Churchill offered
wise words on this: "A pessimist sees the
difficulty in every opportunity; an optimist
sees the opportunity in every difficulty."
Although it is to some degree a character
trait, you can cultivate optimism through
mindful self-reflection, looking back to
past situations and outcomes and how
your responded: perhaps each apparently
negative outcome had its positive side?

TAKE BREAKS

Get into the habit of breaks – from getting out of home or office every couple of hours (at work you could take an indoor walk) to going away at weekends. Any break from a routine or a long session of activity will refresh you. You may feel you don't have time, or people might think less of you, or you just couldn't relax properly. Do it anyway: you'll return to your responsibilities in a stronger, more flexible frame of mind.

ACCEPT DISAPPOINTMENT

Look at any disappointment in the broadest context –
even a year or two-year timescale.
Psychologists recommend this strategy:

*Recognize and express the emotion > Detach yourself >
Re-evaluate your expectations > Zoom out to the bigger
picture > Try again – or re-set your goal*

When trying again, maybe you need to try differently,
or you may get the same result. Altering your direction
might be better than dogged persistence. If you succeed,
you can look back on disappointment as a blessing: a
prompt to a better game-plan.

SEE BEYOND CHALLENGE

We often know that difficulties ahead will test our resilience.
If possible, draw on experience to foresee the time when these
obstacles to peace will be behind you. It can help to think of tough
times as a journey you're on, toward a more relaxing lifestyle.
Meanwhile, find positivity and call upon support wherever you
can. All you can do is your best.

CREATE A SAFE PLACE

Having somewhere to retreat to is a wise
insurance plan. It could be a den in your home
(maybe even a shed or gazebo), a friend's
apartment, a parent's, son's or daughter's spare
room. Sometimes you just need space to sit and
think, or make phone calls. Placing distance
between you and your problem can put it in
perspective. Resorting to your safe place may
alert allies to your need. Remember, you can
bring others here too if it helps. If it's in your own
home, surround yourself with symbols of happy
times, and draw upon their positive energy.

(42)

TUNE INTO NATURE

Nature's healing power is known by people who've adopted a hedgehog, gone wild swimming or tracked migrating birds. It works because our focus is shifted to life elsewhere, away from social stresses. Get out among weather and wildness when you can. In cities, make good use of parks – or take day trips to explore the green periphery. Learn to identify species – this increases your quality of engagement.

Natural harmony

The *Tao Te Ching*, a Chinese classic of the 6th to 4th centuries BC, promotes *wu wei*, or "non-doing". Here are its key principles:

- Do nothing contrary to nature's flow
- Develop easeful awareness – responding to situations as they occur
- Identify and step away from the ego's urges

"We pierce doors and windows to make a house. And it is in these spaces where there is nothing that the house is useful to us."

TAO TE CHING

(43)

WALK YOUR TROUBLES AWAY

The Latin motto *Solvitur ambulando* ("Solve it by walking") should be learned and lived by heart. The rhythm of our own footsteps is literally grounding, and a walker's gradual changes of view counteract the modern emphasis on speed and convenience – especially in the countryside. Be mindful in your walking (focus on sensory experiences) but take the time also to calmly work through any issues you need to resolve.

Walk with a difference

Here are two ways to put an enjoyable spin on walking for relaxation:

- **Choose a focus**
  As a focus for mindfulness on your walk, pick something you're likely to encounter – such as birds, trees, churches, boats – and pay particular attention to your sightings, in a spirit of appreciation. If you combine this with ID, using a field guide or tourist guidebook, so much the better

- **Go mapless**
  If you have plenty of time, getting deliberately lost can be a liberating adventure. Ask passers-by before you consult the map – but always have one (if only on your smartphone) on stand-by. Avoid unsafe areas and getting lost in remote country without a phone signal

CULTIVATE HUMOUR

See if you can put a comic spin on any absurdities that befall you. Approaching life with humour makes neutral or negative events entertaining, and takes the sting out of disappointment. Verbal wit is a gift to others that's amply returned. If you're a good mimic, perform from time to time – avoiding cruelty. Look at things from unusual angles. Make wild connections. Send up your imperfections. Humour strengthens friendship and can inject a flash of warmth into relations with strangers.

EMBRACE CHANGE

Life is an interplay between two types of changes: the ones we seek and the ones that just happen. Deliberate change powers us on the road to fulfilment – unless we're lucky and find ourselves coasting downhill. It's a matter of knowing what you want, spotting the opportunities and following them. Change in our lives, as we tread this path, is a sign we're making a difference, casting off the worst of the familiar to make room for the new.

"They must often change, who would be constant in happiness or wisdom."

CONFUCIUS

Guidelines for change

Follow this action plan for deliberate change:

- **Start small**
  Working through a long list of small changes can be less daunting than a big leap

- **Create a schedule**
  Time cues for particular changes help you stay motivated – they might be calendar-related or prompted by the next time something happens

- **Imagine the outcome**
  A clear picture of what you want to attain can be a great motivation

- **Focus on the positive**
  Invest your energies in cultivating the good rather than eliminating the bad – the bad will be displaced

- **Move forward in stages**
  The cumulative effect of small steps will give you plenty to celebrate

"He who rejects change is the architect of decay."

HAROLD WILSON

AVOID PROCRASTINATION

Delaying decisions often stems from
poor levels of self-esteem or confidence.
As crunch time approaches, you might
panic about making the wrong choice. A
variant of this is having a long-neglected
chore you just can't bring yourself to start.
Either way, you're carrying unnecessary
baggage: the burden of your weakness.
The solution to both situations is to set a
firm schedule for breaking the deadlock.
Build in celebration time too: but first, roll
up your sleeves and take action.

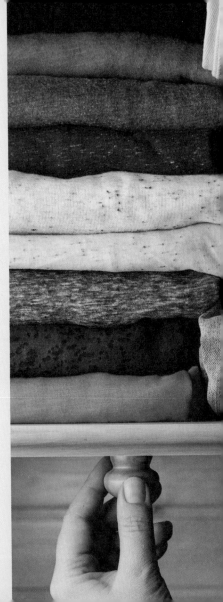

SIMPLIFY YOUR LIFE

Stripping things down to essentials means fewer trivialities to fill your head. Rid yourself of commitments that aren't serving you and are unrelated to your values; rid yourself too of excess *stuff* in the home, which radiates negative energies. A big clear-out will leave you feeling purified, at a deep level – especially if you give away some of your possessions. If you've treasured some things for sentimental reasons, consider donating these too, instead of clinging to the past.

APPRECIATE SOLITUDE

Some dread being alone, but solitude is ideal for
productive self-reflection. It can also provide
relief from social stresses – like a refuge you carry
around with yourself. It's healthy for a couple to
spend separate time alone occasionally. If you have
good relationships, fear of being alone is probably
a symptom of insecurities calling for mindful self-
analysis. Try solo walking, or going alone to a movie,
play or concert – it may grow on you.

*"Salute thyself; see what
thy soul doth wear."*

GEORGE HERBERT

(49)

EXERCISE THE SENSES

We tend to prioritize sight and sound, but making a conscious effort to savour touch, taste and smell enlarges our sensory world, bringing new dimensions of pleasure. Relish textures. Explore the scents of nature in an olfactory safari. Do a mindfulness meditation on something edible and have a multi-sensory experience in the moment. See if you can find words to describe what you've perceived.

RATION DIGITAL LIFE

All aspects of digital technology – but especially social media – can rob us of real-life pleasures. They impose a high opportunity cost. Avoid living too much of your life virtually, exposing yourself too much to digital screens. Beware of becoming an avatar! Set time limits for yourself. Keep sacred boundaries between work and home life: a computer can encourage too leaky a frontier.

(51)

CULTIVATE GRATITUDE

Gratitude is a gesture or attitude of thanks
for what you receive – whether from a person
or from lucky circumstances. An explicit
expression of thanks strengthens your
connection with the giver. To have a grateful
attitude promotes optimism and well-being,
and a sense of belonging. Since gratitude is
a deep love of what has happened, it's deeply
positive. Tell people when you're grateful to
them – it's wrong to imagine you're already
conveying your thanks through subtle signals.

LEARN FROM THE EAST

We've long looked to the East for ideas about the mystery of life and ways to find peace. Buddhism has influenced the West through its wisdom about suffering and impermanence and its emphasis on compassion. It teaches that through mindful attention to ourselves, in meditation, we can triumph over the ego's cravings. Read up on Buddhism and bring its profound insights into your life. Look at Taoism too, with its emphasis on natural flow. And consider taking up an Eastern body practice such as yoga or tai chi.

Eastern promise

Here are some ideas of Eastern thinking.
Explore them in your reading.

- **Karma**
  The Buddhist notion of appropriate consequences originally related to rebirth, but its adaptation in the West as "What goes around comes around" within a single lifetime has created a useful moral compass

- **Nirvana**
  This is ultimate enlightenment – freedom from the cycle of rebirth. Anyone who meditates as a therapeutic exercise can't expect to come near such profound bliss – that would be to misconstrue meditation's purpose. Often the term is used simply as a metaphor for pure joy

- **Awareness**
  This experience takes place when you're wholly present in the moment, without distraction. Only through awareness can real truths be appreciated. The phrase "Be here now", used by yogic practitioner Ram Dass as the title of a popular book, expresses the idea well

- **Tao**
  In Chinese thought the Tao is the "path" or "way", a mystic natural order infusing the cosmos. The *Tao Te Ching*, the ancient sacred text of Taoism, emphasizes paradoxical truths – like the idea that weakness, exemplified by the flexibility of the bamboo, is the best way to be strong

CHAPTER THREE

HAPPILY WORKING

Work is far more than a source of income: it's a crucible in which we help to create ourselves. It provides an outlet for many of our skills and a rich opportunity for learning. It can also expose us to people who may differ from each other more than the people in our friendship group. From our fellow workers we can learn much – not least the value and techniques of teamwork and joint endeavour. Work, however, is a potentially stressful environment; and also there's often the burden of the commute. To defend ourselves against stress we need to strive for a healthy life-work balance, work in accord with our values and be careful not to neglect self-care.

"One of the symptoms of an approaching nervous breakdown is the belief that one's work is terribly important."

BERTRAND RUSSELL

(53)

BALANCE LIFE AND WORK

Alongside health problems, life-work imbalance is the
commonest source of stress in people's lives. Don't let your
home life be compromised too much by work – imagine,
on your journey to and from work, you're entering a
different universe. Inevitably there'll be times when
juggling home life and a busy work schedule will be tricky.
But if you detect signs of stress in yourself, or fracture
lines in your relationships, take remedial action: prioritize
home, self and partner for a while. Explain to your boss:
few would disagree that family is the highest priority.

PUT MONEY IN PERSPECTIVE

Keep money in your head, not in your heart.
Allowing money to define your self-image would
be letting what Carl Jung called the Shadow –
the dark side of the psyche – become dominant.
Acknowledge the emotions often stirred by
money, but don't let them take over your choices.
Steer a way through money worries by placing
faith in your values – and the things you hold
most dear, which are priceless.

*"There are people who have money and
people who are rich."*

COCO CHANEL

DRAW RED LINES

At work we're often pressured into taking on more – the profit motive, in particular, puts a squeeze on workers. Don't try to please your boss by showing you can be superhuman. Define your boundaries – for example, you might resolve to always have a proper lunch break and never stay at work after a certain time. Stick to your guns. Let any displeasure sweep through you and away: it's better than damaging your health or your relationship.

OPTIMIZE YOUR COMMUTE

Commuting can be stressful, especially in the rush hour.
Choose a time, means and route that take the pain out of your
journey. This might mean spending a little more time (for
example, going by bus, not train) for the sake of getting a
seat; or going early. Consider having breakfast after your
commute rather than before. This is an aspect of work you
can control: choose wisely. If you go by car, try to organize
a car share, not least for the sake of the environment.

57

DELEGATE WELL

This is a fundamental of good management. Try to be a good
judge of others' abilities, including ones that may not
currently find an outlet: talk to people and use your
intuition to assess how they can best help, and how much
supervision they'll need. Make it clear to them how helpful
their contribution will be; and thank them regularly. Be
prepared to divert them to other tasks if they're struggling.

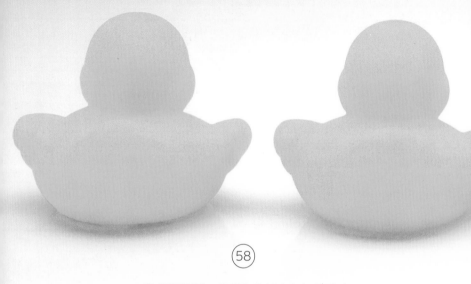

(58)

OFFER ORIGINALITY

The workplace is regulated by tried-and-tested procedures that
may be far from ideal: precedent is no guarantee of excellence.
Be prepared to think outside the box and come up with new ideas that
will benefit all. You may encounter resistance from the old guard. Be
patient in explaining the benefits of any new system. Originality will
be valued, even if not all your innovations can be implemented.

CULTIVATE RELAXED CONFIDENCE

A relaxed confidence style is shown by those who think in the round and are prepared to learn. It stems from well-being. Knowing in detail how your own activity fits in with the total picture is helpful. Insecurity can undermine confidence – particularly fear of job loss or demotion. But if you have a clear view of your own value, such anxieties will affect you less.

VALUE YOUR CONTRIBUTION

A cog-in-a-machine attitude – the belief that your contribution at work is insignificant – can diminish your sense of your own value. But remember, any large enterprise would collapse without its jigsaw of small contributions. It's rewarding to know you're doing good work you can be proud of. If that work is largely routine, it's still worthwhile; and there's value too in the friends you've made at work, and your participation in a complex social organism.

(61)

REJECT "US-AND-THEM" THINKING

Solidarity among workers can be a force for compassionate mutual support and for improving workplace conditions. But the us-and-them culture that sometimes accompanies this can be corrosive. Good communication between different levels of employees has to be better than solid walls that turn bosses and workers into alien species. Build bridges both with your seniors and with staff. Help make the workplace a microcosm of a well-ordered society.

TAKE A PROPER LUNCH BREAK

A conscientious worker may be so focused on the job that lunch gets taken on the wing – with no break from working. Having a sociable lunch in a nearby café is the best option. By all means bring your own packed lunch to work (for economy, if nothing else) but try to consume it away from your desk. If this isn't possible, clear a space, and enjoy your meal slowly, with a glass of water, focusing mindfully on flavours and textures. Go for a 5-minute walk before you start. Do a short breathing meditation, to help mark the beginning of your mealtime.

In tray

DETACH YOURSELF

When problems clutter your in-tray, don't treat this as *personal* pressure. It's your job to deal with such difficulties – part of what you're paid to do. Detach yourself: your work isn't what defines you. If emotions arise at work, think of them as happening within the work part of your brain: don't bring them home with you.

Out tray

BE A TEAM PLAYER

Showing you're an effective team member will win you
credit at work but also brings its own rewards. Show whole-
hearted commitment. Avoid lingering on the sidelines. Be
reliable and flexible – don't insist on sticking to your job
description or allotted role. Also, be a good listener and
communicator. If there's a problem within the team, work
toward a constructive solution without blaming anyone.

FOLLOW A THOUGHTFUL ETHIC

Your work values are part of your identity – as much as the values in your personal life. List them in a charter and put them into practice every day. Be mindfully aware of inevitable small transgressions – everyone will waver occasionally in their commitment or let someone down for understandable reasons. Judge yourself honestly. Learn from your lapses and try to keep them to a minimum in future.

A work value checklist

These ideas offer a starting-point
for your own work value checklist.
Make a copy and display it
by your work station.

- **Prime values**
  Honesty
  Reliability
  Fairness
  Commitment

- **Personal values**
  Leadership
  Communication
  Imagination
  Thoughtfulness

- **Secondary values**
  Punctuality
  Pleasantness
  Meticulousness
  Accuracy

USE APPROPRIATE LANGUAGE

The tone you use at work, in speech, emails and the like, impacts on the way others see you. Even if you're on friendly terms with your boss, keep your language professional in working hours. Avoid misplaced "mirroring": unconsciously adopting the communication style of people you're with. Just be the best version of your self. Remember, swearing radiates negative energy. On gender and minority issues, it's easy to be misunderstood, so err on the safe side.

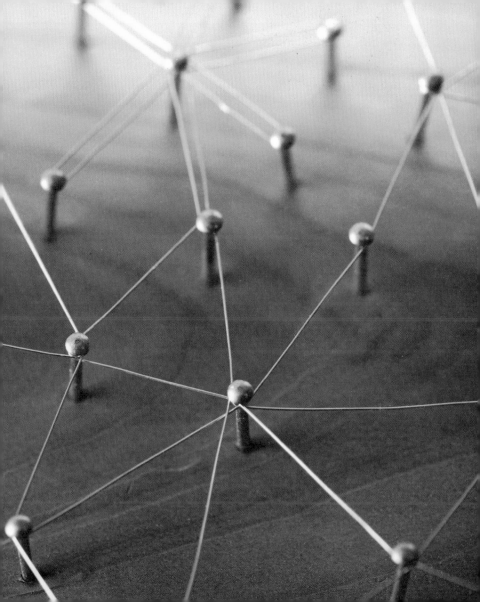

SUPPORT YOUR COLLEAGUES

When workmates openly have difficulties in their personal lives, show your support – if only with a get-well card, a letter, a warm word or two. On work issues, be supportive without getting involved in grievances. Give advice and hands-on assistance when possible – you might need a similar favour some day. If you feel inclined to stand up for a victim of unfair treatment, proceed with care – establish the facts before you act.

(68)

PERSONALIZE
YOUR SPACE

An uninspiring work space stealthily
undermines your mood and creativity.
You can add a personal touch without
sentimentality – having family photos
on your desk is one of countless
options. If you work in your own
box-like module, there's lots of scope
– you could cover the walls, create an
imitation window, install a plant or
two. A rug can help you define your
domain. Avoid cluttering surfaces with
memorabilia – go for maximum
impact with minimum means.

PUT STATUS IN PERSPECTIVE

Status – where we stand in relation to others – means more to
some than salary, though salary too can be seen in status terms.
Even a small increase in status triggers positive emotions. More
important, though, are expertise, competence and experience.
Status follows these in a hit-or-miss way – sometimes influence
operates as well. By all means be ambitious, but focus on genuine
self-development – not lifting yourself up the status ladder
by whatever means you can think of.

LEARN FROM CRITICISM

Criticism often gives a shock to the ego.
Evaluations are common in the modern
workplace, and not all managers will judge you
gently. Don't take criticism personally, even if you
feel it's unfair. If nothing else, it can instruct you
in how you're seen. Perhaps your best qualities are
operating too invisibly? Perhaps there's truth in
what you're being told, even though emotionally
you're resisting it? Say thank you to your assessor.
Ponder later what's been said: see what insights
you can extract and build into your work.

CHAPTER FOUR

HAPPILY CONNECTED

Self-sufficiency is no recipe for a happy life: much of our comfort and stimulation comes from others. At the heart of their social network most adults would identify an intimate partnership, a kinship group and a more fluid collection of friends. Beyond that are neighbours, workmates and more casual acquaintances – people who use, say, the same gym or bus stop. Even the most peripheral contacts can be rewarding – can offer insight, warmth, humour, compassion, moral support, practical help. Three things are needed for us to derive most benefit from our fellow human beings: openness, empathy and communication. With this golden triad we can enrich our lives, overcoming relationship issues and exploring positive experiences we can share.

"Love is the only sane and satisfactory answer to the problem of human existence."

ERICH FROMM

FEEL THE POWER
OF LOVE

We tend to be ambivalent about love. Sometimes the word makes us think about our intimate and family relationships; sometimes we extend the idea to cover friends, writing "love" to sign off emails and cards. In fact, experiencing love for our fellow human beings *en masse* can be one of the foundation stones of a happy life. Like the sun, love is inexhaustible. Let its energy flow from your heart in abundance, displacing its opposites, envy, resentment and indifference.

Loving kindness

Do this Buddhist meditation from time to time to awaken the loving energies inside yourself.

1 Sit comfortably upright in a straight-backed chair, and relax your body and mind

2 Send loving thoughts from your mind to your heart – a surge of self-generated compassion

3 Visualize about six people in turn, and mentally send them your love, as rays from your heart – start with loved ones and progress with diminishing closeness, concluding with someone who dislikes you

(72)

LET GO OF JEALOUSY

"The jealous are a trouble to others,"
William Penn said, "but a torment to
themselves." Jealousy feeds on imagination
taken to extremes. You try to picture
scenarios, but can never be satisfied with
them, since there's no way of ascertaining
their accuracy. Stop torturing yourself.
Remember that jealousy distorts: so use
calm reasoning to come to a better view of
the situation, with all its uncertainties. Avoid
making a big issue of a single suspicious
observation. Don't make undermining
comments. If there are definite signs of
infidelity, express your concerns calmly.
Let your partner have their say. Remember,
forgiveness can be healing.

(73)

FEEL THE POWER
OF TOUCH

Touch is our most direct form of communication
– instant, precious and simple. Make it part of
your vocabulary – a gentle touch on the arm
can be eloquent. You must be sensitive to social
taboos, but even a distant acquaintance may at
times relish the fleeting reassurance of contact.
With friends you can go further: a warm hug
is an exchange of healing energy. Explore too
the therapeutic pleasures of massage, which
warrants a role in any intimate bond.

VALUE EMPATHY

Empathy is breaking through your ego's walls and projecting
yourself into someone else's shoes. It involves intuitively
interpreting tell-tale signs – not just what people say – and
thinking what consequences might stem from someone's difficult
situation. Empathic understanding is the gateway to compassion,
which prompts us to kindness. Make a conscious effort to
understand people and respond to the needs you detect.
Empathy makes all human connection more rewarding.

CELEBRATE ANNIVERSARIES

A birthday or anniversary isn't just a formality: it's the recognition of a person's value to you through time. Rather than just give a card or token present, make it a mutual celebration. Cook a special meal for your loved one, and raise a toast – even if it's just the two of you. As Erich Fromm said, "Love is the only sane and satisfactory answer to the problem of human existence." Use every pretext to affirm its vital energies.

TRY NEW THINGS TOGETHER

Potentially, a romantic partner is an
ally in exciting experiments. Trying a
new leisure, cultural or artistic activity,
or a new way of doing things, can only
deepen your connection. If the experiment
fails, you're more likely to see the funny
side if you've shared the experience; if it
works, you can share happy memories
from two different perspectives – and go
further next time.

(77)

TALK PROBLEMS THROUGH

Festering resentment never resolves relationship issues – it only
makes things worse. Don't wait till the next row to explore the
issues: emotions will probably be running too high for problem-
solving. Schedule a discussion, allowing ample time. Choose a
neutral setting – a café or restaurant. Agree you'll both approach
the chat in a constructive spirit, to reach a mutually acceptable
conclusion. There's a lot you can do together before you even
think about going to a counsellor. Don't expect a definitive
solution – just agreement on the way forward.

Communication signposts

Here are some pointers for good communication in a close relationship:

- **Reason within reason**
  When your partner is talking about emotions, apply empathy, not reason. Don't argue they're being irrational. Explore the emotions together

- **Listen and learn**
  Don't be so engaged with your own ideas that you don't accept something that doesn't conform with them. Learn from feedback. Thank your partner for their honesty

- **Accept change**
  Don't expect your partner not to have evolved in their needs and priorities since you first got together. Work out how any new elements can be accommodated within your bond

(78)

GIVE YOUR PARTNER SPACE

A healthy relationship is not a glue keeping two people in permanent togetherness. If you each follow your own interests, with your own friendships, this will strengthen trust and bring variety to your conversations. However, don't be rigid about boundaries: let him/her into your domain at times. Periods of solitude will also help to enhance mutual well-being.

79

NEGOTIATE LIGHTLY

In any negotiation, try to be relaxed and friendly,
even when the subject is serious – and even
when you encounter coolness or brusqueness.
A light tone is helpful, and doesn't prevent you
from sticking to your points. Make it clear you
offer trust, as this makes for better outcomes.
Use gentle humour (but not at the other's
expense!): if you can get someone to smile,
confrontation is less likely.

80

GIVE THOUGHTFUL CARE

The poet Maya Angelou devised a
good motto for carers: "Be a rainbow in
someone else's cloud."
For sure, caregiving can be stressful, but
also rewarding, bringing new closeness
to a relationship. The key is being
sensitive to each other's needs. Give care
mindfully, focusing on the moment.
Listen, and value what you learn. Allow
your dependant to make their own
decisions. Spring pleasant surprises.
Be sure to take time off for
your own interests and friends.

BE A GOOD NEIGHBOUR

You can live next door to someone and know nothing about them. But in fact neighbours offer a valuable chance, paradoxically, of extending your horizons while making your area more sociable. Introduce yourself and stay in touch. Set up (or join) an email or other online network to share local news and useful contacts. Look out for each other. Keep noise down and be thoughtful about parties, indoors or out, and the state of your yard. Deal with disputes in a responsible way. Respect the wishes of those who want to keep a friendly distance.

FACE FACTS TOGETHER

We all create myths about ourselves, for self-protection. When a couple both subscribe to the same myth (such as pretending that they're happy for appearances' sake, that damaging behaviour on one side is acceptable or that they can afford their lifestyle), the prospects for happiness are diminished. Avoid engaging in a tacit collusion to stay quiet about the biggest difficulties. Face them together, in a mutually supportive, problem-solving spirit.

MANAGE ANGER

When someone lets anger take them over, the ensuing firestorm may suck in other people. Try to detach yourself and not get angry yourself, however unreasonable their behaviour. Think of yourself as a fire fighter behind a protective helmet: your priority is not to catch fire yourself. If you're prompted to speak, do so in moderate tones and be specific – general statements such as "I hear what you're saying" will not be soothing. Try to make a helpful, concrete suggestion. If you're the angry one, the sooner you notice this the better. Pull back and see the situation as if through a window. Count to 10 while breathing deeply.

FORGIVE OTHERS

When your heart hardens against someone
who has hurt you, you dose yourself with pain
and poison. Consider what might be holding
back your forgiveness. Rather than dwelling
on past wrongs, let people show their best
qualities, now and in the future. Allow them
back into your life in a refreshed relationship.
Any ray of forgiveness we send out reflects
back to us and makes us stronger.

CULTIVATE KINDNESS

Kindness prompted by empathy benefits the giver as well as the
recipient, for it enlarges your sense of self-worth. The 14th Dalai
Lama has said of kindness, "It is always possible," which is more
profound than it might initially seem. Try performing five random
acts of kindness in a day, or over a couple of days. Ask people
what they need, so you can target your giving effectively. Give
a present for no particular reason from time to time.

(86)

NOURISH ALLIANCES

Our network of family and friends is potentially a safety net – to catch us when we lose our footing. Yet many who face challenges prefer to battle in silence rather than show vulnerability by reaching out. True friends will be only too happy to help: don't hesitate to unburden yourself. Be sure to choose the ally you need – whether it's someone empathic who's good at listening, a clear thinker who'll help you cut through muddles or a supportive champion to speak or act on your behalf.

SPEAK UP FOR YOURSELF

There can be reasons for staying quiet
even when it's in your best interests to
speak. You may feel you're outnumbered
or your thoughts are too complex to
convey clearly, or you may doubt your own
persuasive powers. You might lack self-
confidence or self-worth or be reluctant to
inconvenience or detain others by raising
an obstacle. It can be particularly difficult
to speak after you've been silent a long
time. But you're more likely to regret not
speaking than speaking. Get into the habit
of calmly, unemphatically expressing your
point of view. Be opinionated – in a good
way. Your opinion counts.

CHAPTER FIVE

HAPPILY BUSY

Few of us use our downtime just to put our feet up: instead, we pursue activities of our choice, keeping minds and bodies occupied. We're driven to extend both our knowledge and experience. We feel happiest when we fill our roles in rewarding ways and follow our paths with measurable progress – as mother, friend, householder, worker, gardener, artist or whatever. Above all, we value having a purpose, and the whole notion of purpose is inconceivable without activity. A purpose that keeps us rewardingly busy for a significant proportion of our time gives meaningful shape to our lives.

"The best way to lengthen out our days is to walk steadily and with a purpose."

CHARLES DICKENS

KEEP LEARNING

Learning gives you a sense of purpose –
especially if you set targets along the way. It
enlarges your mind, even if you're learning
something practical such as printmaking or
car mechanics; this in turn enhances your
relationships with others. Whatever your
chosen subject, you'll enhance your "soft
personal skills" such as self-regulation, social
adaptability and good communication. At
the same time, your confidence to try new
things and stretch yourself will grow.

89

ENTER THE ZONE

It's a principle of positive psychology to value activities that
engage your whole attention in the moment. This is the "flow"
state, or Zone. You can enter it via any endeavour demanding
concentration – from playing chess to pruning roses. Fully
absorbed, you lose the sense of time passing. People who often
enter this state tend to concentrate better and have higher
self-worth. Throw yourself into whatever interests you:
the reward is complete mental refreshment.

90

NOURISH YOUR TALENTS

Knowing what you're good at is
just as beneficial as knowing your
weaknesses. Don't let modesty
obscure your sense of your own skill-
set – why eclipse a large part of who
you are? Knowing your talents puts
you in a position to develop them
further, making yourself exceptional.
Build on what you can do, so you end
up being capable of even more.

HAVE A PROJECT

A project is a long-term commitment to attain an end – often something physical, like a garden makeover, but sometimes intangible, such as fluency in another language. You have a relationship with your project: you make a commitment to it. As if it were a person, you might at times neglect it and feel guilty – on your own behalf. In fact, a person could *be* a project – for example, if you teach someone literacy. The value of any personal venture is the sense of purpose it gives you. This enriches your life.

CELEBRATE THE EVERYDAY

Many of us dream of travel, and make that dream reality from time to time if we're fortunate. But there are countless enriching experiences to be found on our own doorsteps and within our everyday routines. The starting-point is mindful attention: noticing your surroundings. Track the seasons – the first migrant birds, the first frosts. Every day holds surprises: register them with relish.

An everyday safari

Stay on the lookout for any of these ordinary blessings. Write up the most striking examples in your diary. Give thanks for them in your imagination.

- Cloud patterns and weather
- Amazing fashion choices
- Overheard conversations
- Chance encounters
- Moments of humour
- Incongruous pairings

"To be interested in the changing seasons is a happier state of mind than to be hopelessly in love with spring."

GEORGE SANTAYANA

KEEP AND MEND

Resisting wasteful consumerism is a commendable principle. We know the throwaway culture is bad for our planet. It's also counter to the Stoic idea of nourishing contentment by making do with less. If you're able to keep an old garment, tool, device or furnishing item – perhaps after repair or adjustment – instead of replacing it, you can take pride in following a long tradition of thrift and keeping your carbon footprint small. Learn mending skills such as darning if you don't already have them. If you do need to dispose of things, favour giving them away over recycling.

PICTURE GOOD OUTCOMES

When you embark on a project or plan for personal change, motivation can flag at times, however good your intentions. When aiming for a long-term goal, use creative visualization to picture the desired outcome in detail. Imagine how the moment will feel, to all the senses. A mental picture of this kind will transmit empowering energy into your heart.

FOLLOW DIVERSIONS

Taking a by-way you hadn't planned to follow, you may come across unexpected rewards. This is true both literally and metaphorically. Whatever objectives you're pursuing, be open to the idea of a diversion when the chance presents itself. You might even decide to change your main direction of travel. Of course, distraction can be a pretext for procrastination: be aware of this pitfall. But as long as you're not neglecting anything important, feel free to wander. Enjoy your encounters along the way.

"A straight path never leads anywhere except to the objective."

ANDRÉ GIDE

96

START YOUR DAY EARLY

The morning is a time of golden promise. Rising early every day, and even earlier once or twice a week, sets you up well for anything ahead. If there are difficulties to face, you can prepare for them – maybe with a meditation. Doing something special, such as walking in the park or listening to an interesting podcast, gives colour to an ordinary day and is particularly refreshing if you then go to work. Think of the hour before everyone else gets up as a gift from the universe.

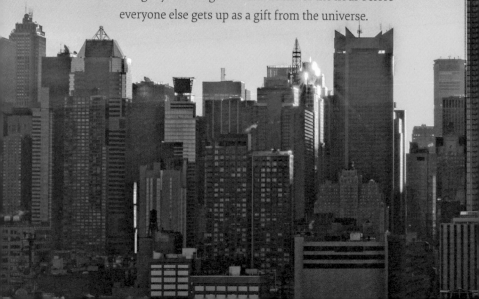

"The breeze at dawn has secrets to tell you.
Don't go back to sleep."

RUMI

GET INVOLVED

It's empowering and mind-
expanding to participate in local
affairs. Busy yourself in the
backroom decisions that impact
on your life and that of your
neighbours. Make your voice
heard on others' behalf. Being
a community activist can be hard
work but it's a good feeling to know
you're making a difference.

The value of curiousity

Curiosity is the sign of lively engagement with the world and with others, and of an eagerness to learn and be surprised. All this makes it a virtue. The curious enrich themselves, inwardly, through pleasurable discoveries. They also make good company. Once embarked on the path of curiosity, you'll soon come across fascinating connections, prompting you to explore further. Keep boredom at bay by honing your antennae to probe into fascinating corners. This is where true treasures lie.

98

EXPRESS YOURSELF THROUGH HOME

Lavishing attention on the home, to make it comfortable, attractive and personalized, is a form of self-care, with many benefits. A haven you've actively enhanced becomes an even more congenial and relaxing place to be. By expressing what you like about your own personality, it reinforces your self-worth. You can magnify the effect by surrounding yourself with mementoes of happy times – family portraits, objects picked up on your travels. A well-tended house or apartment is the perfect place for entertaining too. Your home is a blank canvas – fill it with imagination and your personal style.

SCRIBBLE AWAY

Writing down your thoughts and feelings is the
perfect vehicle for self-exploration. You needn't
think of this as creative writing – maybe more
as a verbal mirror to see yourself more clearly.
This is a good way to help you understand
the issues you face, and explore your own and
other peoples' emotions. Start a journal: fill it
in regularly. Reading back your entries, you can
trace your emotional development and identify
repeated triggers and responses. Consider
also doing more freestyle, no-holds-barred
scribbling in "morning pages" before or after
breakfast – this can be therapeutic.

BE A MENTOR

Teaching can be a kind of inverse learning. A responsive pupil
gives a great deal back – not least an enthusiasm that may instil
in the teacher a new joy in his or her subject. You can be a mentor
at any age, but it's particularly rewarding in later life, when there's
accumulated experience to convey. A young student can provide
the occasion for a bridge across generations. Set expectations
and ground rules before you start (including a contact schedule);
assess the pupil's needs; work together with mutual commitment
toward agreed goals. Allow yourself plenty of listening time –
don't just hold forth. Let the pupil make decisions, even ones
you might not have made yourself in their position.

PLAN FOR RETIREMENT

Retired people enjoy an above-average portion
of happiness: free time liberates body and mind.
However, loss of the purpose and companionship
often found, even unconsciously, at work can
come as a shock; and you may need to adjust to a
new dynamic with your partner. Before leaving
employment, explore ways to continue living
purposefully and sociably. Volunteering
or freelancing can help fill the gap.